YIKES!
IT'S HAUNTED

Educational Media

Carson Dellosa Education
Greensboro, North Carolina

Rourke Educational Media
Carson Dellosa Education
PO Box 35665
Greensboro, NC 27425 USA

Printed in the USA • All rights reserved.   ISBN 978-1-4838-5464-9
01-140198313

TABLE OF CONTENTS

PARENT LETTER

Dear Parents and Caregivers,

Yikes! It's Haunted will thrill your young reader with spooky tales of haunted buildings, mysterious happenings, eerie locations, and more. Each 30-page section explores one type of place or object that is believed to be haunted.

Before reading, ask your child what he or she already knows about each topic. If there is a map at the beginning of the section, look at it together, talking about each place shown in relation to the location of your home. Talk about ghosts and the paranormal: What are your child's thoughts about whether things or places can be haunted? Are these beliefs based on facts, feelings, or both? Does your child expect to read information that will support or challenge his or her ideas?

During reading, encourage your child to stop when he or she comes to an unfamiliar word. Provide a print or online dictionary for looking up the meaning of each new word. Challenge your child to state the definition in his or her own words and use it in a sentence. Be sure to express interest when your child points out an especially vivid photo or an astonishing bit of information from the book. Celebrate your child's curiosity and let these haunted tales spark open-ended discussion.

After reading, ask your child to summarize what he or she learned about each topic. Which haunting was the spookiest? Which story was most or least believable? How much of the text was based on facts that can be proven? Use the comprehension questions provided on pages 185–187 to help. As a follow-up to reading this book, your child might be inspired to write a new collection of spooky stories or haunting reports.

Happy reading!
Rourke Educational Media

YIKES! IT'S HAUNTED

GRAVEYARDS

AUTHOR: ALEX SUMMERS

TABLE OF CONTENTS

HAUNTED BATTLEFIELDS AND CEMETERIES OF THE WORLD

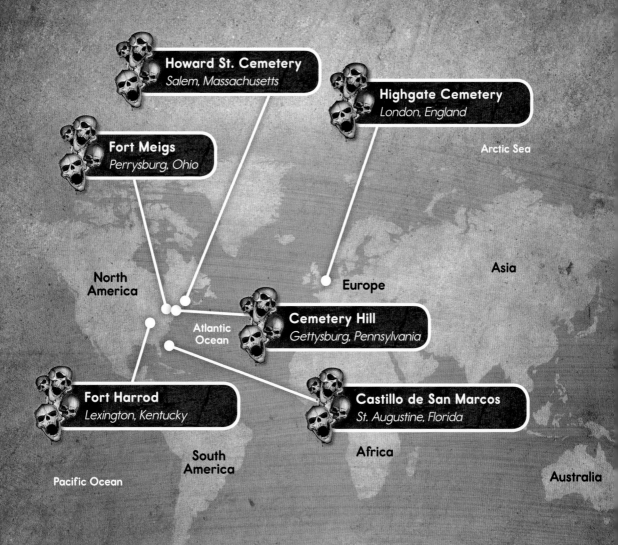

Howard St. Cemetery
Salem, Massachusetts

Highgate Cemetery
London, England

Fort Meigs
Perrysburg, Ohio

Arctic Sea

North America

Asia

Europe

Atlantic Ocean

Cemetery Hill
Gettysburg, Pennsylvania

Fort Harrod
Lexington, Kentucky

Castillo de San Marcos
St. Augustine, Florida

South America

Africa

Australia

Pacific Ocean

Southern Ocean

SCARY PLACES, SCARY FACES!

Cemeteries are burial grounds for the dead. Battlefields are **combat** sites where many lives have been lost.

READ IT

Paranormal research involves looking for evidence of supernatural activity. This type of activity is not explained by science or the laws of nature.

Cemeteries and battlefields have been known to have a lot of paranormal, or unexplained, activity. These strange **phenomena** can make you think, "Yikes! It's haunted!"

Many believe that when people die, especially in a violent way, their spirits sometimes stay at the location of their death.

The spirits may not understand why they are stuck there, but they make themselves known in different ways. Some of their **tactics** are hair-raising!

▶▶ Sometimes paranormal investigators try to help ghosts cross over to the spirit world.

Are these spirits friendly? Not always. Some are tormented and show themselves in frightening ways to people who visit these sites.

CEMETERY HILL

Cemetery Hill in Gettysburg, Pennsylvania, saw some of the bloodiest battles during the Battle of Gettysburg in 1863.

▶▶ Cemetery Hill, just outside of Gettysburg, is where most of the soldiers tragically met their end.

READ IT

So many people died in this famous battle that it was impossible to get them all buried before the stench of rotting death filled the air. The smells lasted so long, people could not walk near the cemetery without holding handkerchiefs dipped in peppermint and vanilla over their noses. Visitors still report smelling these scents to this day.

▶▶ The energy from the three-day battle is said to still linger. For the souls that remain, the battle continues.

Many people have reported seeing ghosts walking the Hill. They say these ghosts touch them in angry ways as if demanding they leave.

Highgate Cemetery in North London, England, is said to be one of the world's most haunted cemeteries. Many famous people are buried there. It is known for the ghosts who haunt it as well as the many **sinister** activities reported to occur at the site.

▶▶ It is not the notable names buried at Highgate Cemetery that make it so mystifying; it's the non-living entities that seem to reside in the burial grounds alongside them.

The Highgate Vampire is said to stand more than seven feet tall with piercing, hypnotic eyes. Visitors report he wears a long black cape and top hat and vanishes into thin air.

▶▶ **The cemetery's grounds are full of mature trees and spooky gravestones.**

READ IT

Many people have reported spine-chilling events occurring at Highgate. The cemetery's history and reputation have made it one of the most visited places in the United Kingdom for people who like to experience paranormal activity.

DARK DESTINATION!
HOWARD STREET CEMETERY

Howard Street Cemetery in Salem, Massachusetts, is famous for the Salem Witch Trials. Its most famous ghost is Giles Corey. He was the only victim of the trials that was **tortured** to death for neither admitting nor defending his innocence.

▶▶ There are more than 300 gravestones at the historic Howard Street Cemetery.

Giles died as a result of "pressing." They placed large, heavy stones on top of him, trying to provoke a confession. In the end, he did not confess and his last words were, "More weight, more weight."

▶▶ Giles Corey was 80 years old when he was accused of witchcraft. On September 19, 1692, Corey was tortured and killed in the back part of what is now Howard Street Cemetery.

HAUNTED BATTLEFIELDS

Still standing in St. Augustine, Florida, Castillo de San Marcos is one of the most haunted forts in the world. Built by the Spaniards and completed in 1702, this former military **fortress** saw a lot of action.

▶▶ Castillo de San Marcos, or "The Old Fort" to locals, draws visitors from all over the world. If you are a ghost hunter, or simply want to experience an area that is known for its true ghost stories, a trip to "The Old Fort" is an absolute must!

Many people were captured and died here throughout the battles it withstood, leaving plenty of opportunities for spirits to linger.

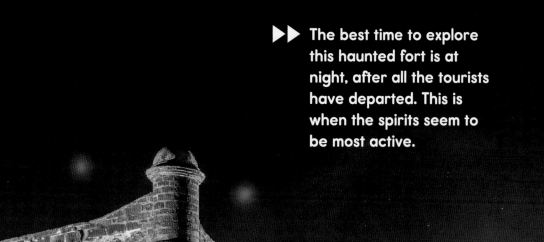

▶▶ **The best time to explore this haunted fort is at night, after all the tourists have departed. This is when the spirits seem to be most active.**

READ IT

The most haunted areas of the fort are said to be the dungeon and the soldiers' quarters. Orbs, the sounds of soldier's boots, and an apparition of a soldier seen walking through the castle with a lantern are just a few of the spooky sights and sounds you may experience there.

Fort Meigs, built in 1813, is located in Perrysburg, Ohio. A place of **bloodshed** and battle, it is the perfect spot for hauntings. And that is just what you will find.

▶▶ **The blockhouses that are around the fort are especially haunted. It is said that if you are in there, sometimes you can hear the footsteps of the soldiers walking around. Others have said that while walking outside of a blockhouse, they can see figures in the windows watching them.**

READ IT

There are at least three unmarked cemeteries in the Fort Meigs area. One of them is a Native American burial ground. Many lives were lost among the Americans, British, and Native Americans during the battles. It is estimated that up to 500 bodies are buried under and around the fort.

Visitors report hearing the sound of cannon and musket fire at night. Sometimes they hear fifes and drums—as if the soldiers entering battle are still alive!

MAJOR AMOS STODDARD
1762 — 1813

WOUNDED MAY 1 1813. ON THE OPENING DAY OF THE SIEGE OF FORT MEIGS, DIED MAY 11 OF TETANUS, BURIED MAY 12 IN FRONT OF THE "GRAND BATTERY" ON THE SPOT, WHERE HE RECEIVED THE WOUND THAT CAUSED HIS DEATH.

A NATIVE OF CONNECTICUT, MAJOR STODDARD SERVED IN THE AMERICAN REVOLUTION, PRACTICED LAW IN MASSACHUSETTS, AND BECAME A MEMBER OF THE MASSACHUSETTS LEGISLATURE. HE ENTERED THE U.S. ARMY IN 1798 AS A CAPTAIN IN THE SECOND REGIMENT OF ARTILLERISTS AND ENGINEERS. COMMISSIONED THE FIRST CIVIL AND MILITARY COMMANDANT OF UPPER LOUISIANA HE RECEIVED THAT TERRITORY FROM THE FRENCH IN 1804 IN THE NAME OF THE UNITED STATES.

HE WAS PROMOTED TO THE RANK OF MAJOR IN 1807 AND COMMANDED THE ARTILLERY AT FORT MEIGS WHEN HE WAS WOUNDED.

▶▶ Apparitions are also seen. Most of them are reported to be the American soldiers who stayed at the fort.

21

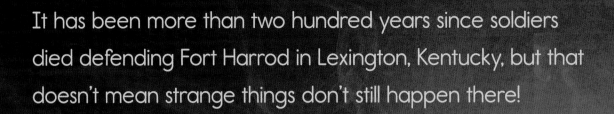

It has been more than two hundred years since soldiers died defending Fort Harrod in Lexington, Kentucky, but that doesn't mean strange things don't still happen there!

READ IT

Cabins adjoining the fort are usually occupied by re-enactors, people who dress up in period clothing and replay battles for visitors. These people have expressed fear of being alone in the area. They also report feeling as though someone is always watching them. Demonic voices have also been heard in the adjoining conference hall. There is no shortage of paranormal activity at this haunted fortress.

22

The original fort is gone, but replicas now stand next to the cemetery where the fallen soldiers rest, the names on their grave markers long since washed away.

▶▶ Heinous deaths were a common occurrence at the fort. Many believe their tortured souls remain.

WHAT CAUSES A HAUNTING?

Though there may be different reasons a spirit attaches to a place, hauntings seem to have a few things in common.

▶▶ Old buildings have seen a lot of history and chances are people have died there, sometimes in violent ways, making them hot spots for wandering spirits to roam.

A very old place that has a long history of human use is more likely to be haunted than a newer one. The longer a place exists, the higher the chance that bad things have happened there.

▶▶ Research shows that hauntings are more frequent at places that have been used for multiple purposes over the years.

Many ghost hunters, or people that **investigate** the paranormal, think spirits haunt places that are filled with strong negative emotions in order to tell the story of that area to people who are still alive.

▶▶ Spirits may show themselves as a way of asking for help.

This is why these spirits tend to haunt places that are the source of their personal pain and **sufferings**. They want others to know their own story in that location.

▶▶ **Some believe that people who die young remain tied to the living world because they don't want to leave their families.**

READ IT

Revealing themselves in their former state is a way for spirits to let others know who they were and lead people into an investigation of the spirit's personal past since their presence indicates that their previous life was not average, normal, or filled with happiness.

Most ghosts seem to appear in a form that resembles the figure that they had in life, so living people can see them as they once were.

▶▶ When people report seeing apparitions such as someone in a wedding dress, it can often be proven that at some point during the history of the location, a death occurred there that involved such a person.

This desire to let the living know of their past hardships and problems means that the ghosts really will reveal themselves to all kinds of people.

Sometimes at their time of death, they had unfinished business of great importance to them. The spirit may urgently want to contact loved ones still here on Earth.

▶▶ Cold chills, your hair standing up on end, the sensation of someone's hand on you when no one is there ... some believe these sensations are caused by a spirit trying to communicate.

▶▶ Ghost tours and overnight stays at haunted locations have become popular activities for people interested in the paranormal.

If your imagination gets the best of you, maybe you could do some paranormal investigations of your own, or plan a family trip to a nearby haunted location. Even if you don't believe in ghosts now, you never know what might change your mind!

31

What do you believe?

GLOSSARY

bloodshed (BLUHD-shed): the injury or killings of human beings, particularly as a result of a war or battle

combat (KAHM-bat): fighting between people or armies

fortress (FOR-tris): a place such as a castle that is protected from attack

investigate (in-VES-ti-gate): to gather information about something or someone

phenomena (fuh-NAH-muh-nah): something very unusual and remarkable

sinister (SIN-uh-stuhr): having an evil appearance, looking likely to cause something harmful or dangerous to happen

sufferings (SUHF-uh-reens): the result of undergoing painful or discomforting events

tactics (TAK-tiks): plans or methods to win a battle or achieve a goal

tortured (TOR-churd): to have endured extreme pain or mental suffering as punishment or as a way to force someone to tell or do something

INDEX

YIKES! IT'S HAUNTED

PRISONS

AUTHOR: ALEX SUMMERS

TABLE OF CONTENTS

HAUNTED PRISONS AND ASYLUMS OF THE WORLD

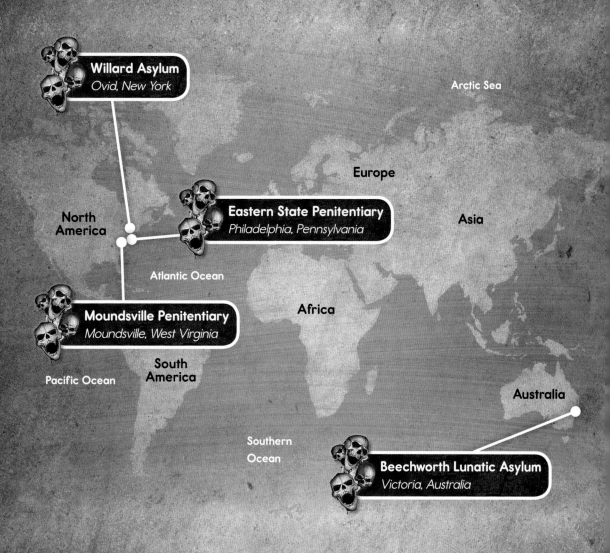

Willard Asylum
Ovid, New York

Arctic Sea

Europe

Asia

North America

Eastern State Penitentiary
Philadelphia, Pennsylvania

Atlantic Ocean

Africa

Moundsville Penitentiary
Moundsville, West Virginia

South America

Pacific Ocean

Australia

Southern Ocean

Beechworth Lunatic Asylum
Victoria, Australia

GHOSTLY PRISONS AND THE HAUNTED INSANE!

Prisons house people convicted of committing a crime. **Asylums** held mentally ill people. But the two have more in common than you may think!

READ IT

Hundreds of years ago, it was thought that mentally ill people did something wrong to lose control of their minds. Instead of medical treatment, they were shamed and punished. Asylums were built to keep these people away from society.

Torture, inhumane treatment, and other horrors have been documented at prisons and asylums throughout history.

Gruesome and violent deaths occurred at these places over the years.

Many think the spirits of these tortured people never left these buildings.

▶▶ Just thinking about the torture people experienced at these places is enough to make you shiver even without seeing a ghost.

Some prisons and asylums are famous for their paranormal, or unexplained, activity. Spirits are said to make their presence known in frightening and violent ways. Enter one of these places and you're likely to think, "Yikes! It's haunted!"

▶▶ **In order for a ghost or spirit to appear, it requires energy, according to paranormal researchers. It will draw heat from its surroundings, or you, to manifest itself.**

READ IT

Paranormal research involves looking for evidence of supernatural activity. This type of activity is not explained by science or the laws of nature.

MOUNDSVILLE PENITENTIARY

This gothic, castle-like penitentiary in West Virginia opened in 1876. Built to hold 480 prisoners, at times it held up to 2,400. These people were often cruelly tortured in strange and unusual ways.

▶▶ **The West Virginia Penitentiary reached its peak population during the 1960s. The last 35 years of the prison, from 1960 - 1995, had many disturbances, including riots and escapes.**

With its violent past and deplorable conditions, many spirits are thought to still reside here. It is a hot spot for those who study paranormal activity.

▶▶ **The mad chair bound a person so tightly, it cut off circulation to their limbs. Amputations were often required afterward.**

READ IT

The Kicking Jenny and the Shoo-Fly were just a couple of instruments used to inflict extreme pain on prisoners. Inmates would be tied bent over on the Kicking Jenny so their skin was pulled tight and then whipped bloody. The Shoo-Fly, an extreme form of water-boarding, used a hose turned on full blast against the inmate's face.

The hangings, murders, and cruel **methods** used to kill or punish inmates caused the prison to be closed in 1995. But not everyone has left. There are many souls said to linger throughout the prison.

READ IT

The most reported paranormal activity occurs in the chapel, the Sugar Shack, and at the north wagon gate, where prisoners were led from their cells to their impending death. The circular entrance gate, where prisoners were brought into the prison, is said to mysteriously turn as if unseen spirits are still entering.

According to popular legend, the prison buildings were built on an old Native American burial ground. Some believe the legend coupled with its violent past makes it a prime spot for the paranormal. Visit if you dare, but be prepared to be SCARED!

▶▶ Ghost hunters and paranormal researchers often stay overnight at these places. Yikes!

EASTERN STATE PENITENTIARY

Eastern State Penitentiary in Philadelphia, Pennsylvania, is not only one of the nation's creepiest prisons, it is also one of its top haunted attractions.

▶▶ Cell block 12 is known for echoing voices and cackling; Cell block 6 for shadowy figures darting along the walls; Cell block 4 for visions of ghostly faces. No wonder it's considered one of the most haunted places in the world.

Started as a Quaker prison in 1892 to reform prisoners, it was the first prison to use solitary confinement.

47

This form of punishment didn't go so well. Many of the prisoners who were exposed to this twisted form of abuse were driven to insanity and then punished by prison **staff**.

READ IT

Every fall, the prison spooks fear-seekers with an event called "Terror Behind the Walls," a sinister tour that features six extravagant sets and 200 ghostly actors.

Closed in 1971, walking through the prison's decaying **corridors** now is like walking through a spine-chilling, spirit-filled horror house!

▶▶ Its 142-year history is full of suicide, madness, disease, murder, and torture, making it easy to imagine the spirits of troubled souls left behind to roam its abandoned halls.

BEECHWORTH LUNATIC ASYLUM

Beechworth is located in northern Victoria, Australia. It is situated at the top of a hill. Just the sight of the building will give you chills!

In the cellar, the spirit of a man is said to appear only to vanish in a split second right before your eyes. Matron Sharpe, who spent most of her life there, has been spotted roaming the halls as if looking for a way out.

READ IT

Now a decommissioned psychiatric hospital, it was closed in 1995 after 128 years of operation. Currently owned by La Trobe University, ghost tours are held at the old asylum, allowing the public access to the most haunted areas said to be filled with spirits of former patients.

Mysterious screams are heard and doors swing open and closed by themselves. A woman is often photographed standing in the window she was reportedly thrown out of by other inmates.

▶▶ The ghost of a Jewish patient who was thrown to her death for a pack of cigarettes is reported to appear at the spot where she fell.

Beechworth Asylum opened in 1867. The vast hospital housed as many as 1,200 patients. More than 9,000 patients are thought to have died here.

Paranormal investigators and the people who tour Beechworth all conclude that the entire place has a certain spine-tingling **eeriness** about it.

Not a place you'd want to be in alone at night. Or is it?

53

HAUNTED WILLARD ASYLUM

In 1869, the Willard Asylum for the Chronic Insane was opened, named after Dr. Willard in Ovid, New York. During the 1800s in America, the mentally ill were not treated kindly. If unable to afford private care, they were forced into poorhouses where their conditions often worsened.

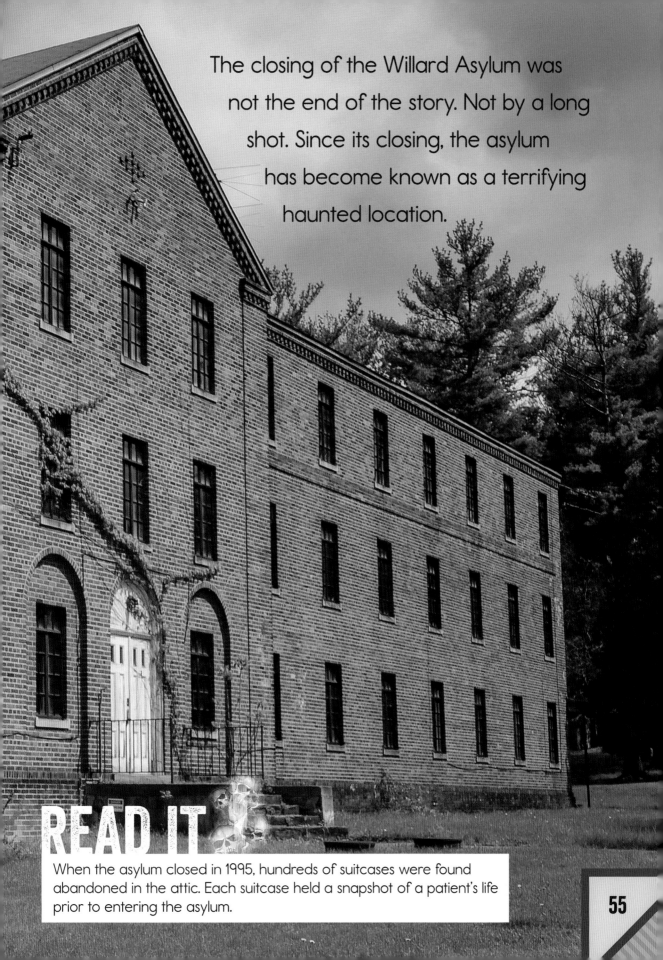

The closing of the Willard Asylum was not the end of the story. Not by a long shot. Since its closing, the asylum has become known as a terrifying haunted location.

READ IT

When the asylum closed in 1995, hundreds of suitcases were found abandoned in the attic. Each suitcase held a snapshot of a patient's life prior to entering the asylum.

Former patients have been seen roaming the halls. Unexplained screams and moans seem to echo from all over the asylum.

READ IT

The Willard Asylum has been investigated on several ghost hunting shows, including *Paranormal State* and *Destination Fear*.

Visitors have also reported seeing the **apparition** of a red-haired woman. This spirit is thought to be a former nurse who became a patient of Willard Asylum. Maybe she is still looking for patients to care for ... or maybe she wants to care for the visitors!

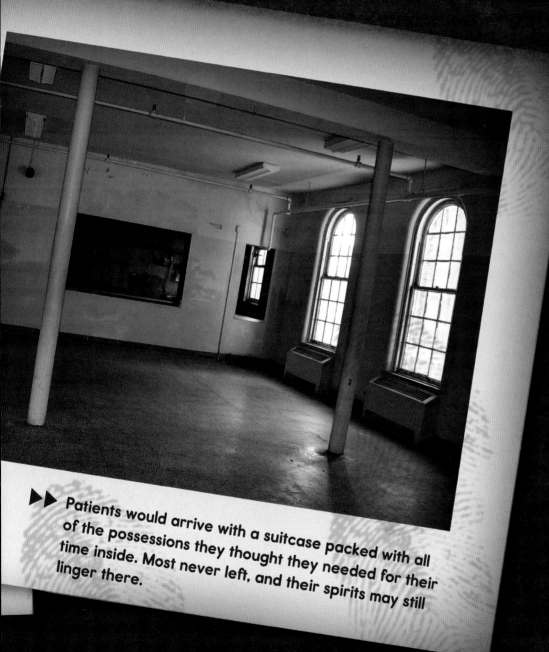

▶▶ Patients would arrive with a suitcase packed with all of the possessions they thought they needed for their time inside. Most never left, and their spirits may still linger there.

WHAT CAUSES A HAUNTING?

Many people believe haunted places exist, but why? Most haunted places have ghostly residents with extensive stories about why their spirits linger in a particular place.

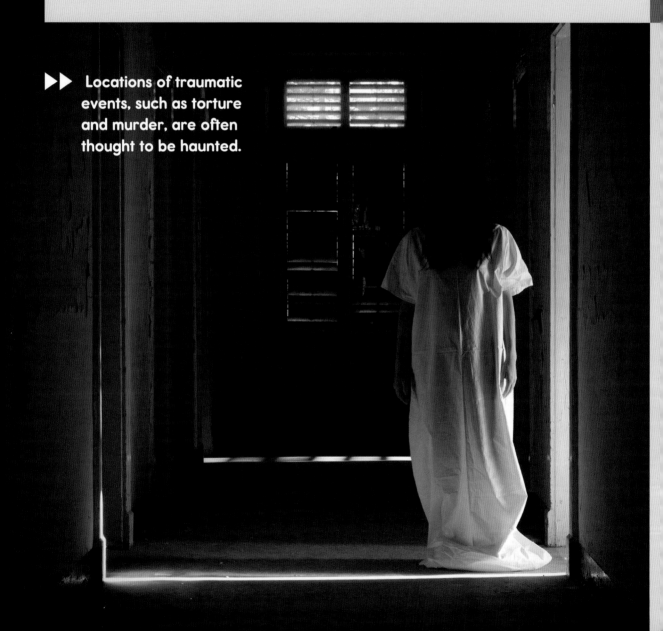

▶▶ Locations of traumatic events, such as torture and murder, are often thought to be haunted.

Some places tend to draw ghosts because of the events that took place there. Prisons and asylums are favorite haunting areas for the **departed**.

Bad events or situations are thought to increase the probability of a haunting in a certain location.

Violent deaths, cruelty, and abuse are some of the most prominent events thought to bind a ghost to the **earthly** realm.

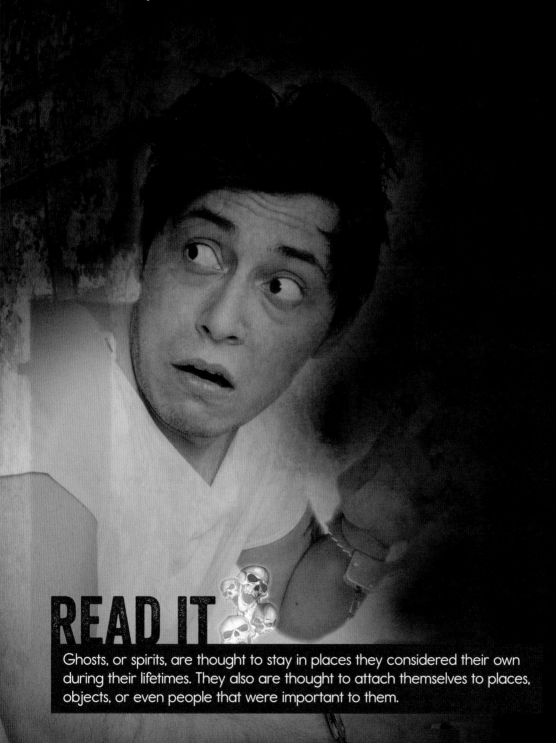

READ IT

Ghosts, or spirits, are thought to stay in places they considered their own during their lifetimes. They also are thought to attach themselves to places, objects, or even people that were important to them.

What do you believe?

GLOSSARY

apparition (AH-puh-ri-shuhn): a ghost or ghost-like image of a person

asylums (uh-SYE-luhms): hospitals for people who are mentally ill and cannot live on their own

corridors (KOR-i-duhrz): long hallways or passages in a building

departed (di-PAHRT-id): to have left, died, or moved on

earthly (urth-LEE): of or relating to the Earth or human life on the Earth

eeriness (EER-ee-nuhs): strangely spooky

methods (METH-uhds): particular ways of doing things

staff (staf): a group of people who work for an institution

INDEX

YIKES! IT'S HAUNTED

HOTELS

AUTHOR: GRACE RAMSEY

TABLE OF CONTENTS

HAUNTED HOTELS OF THE WORLD

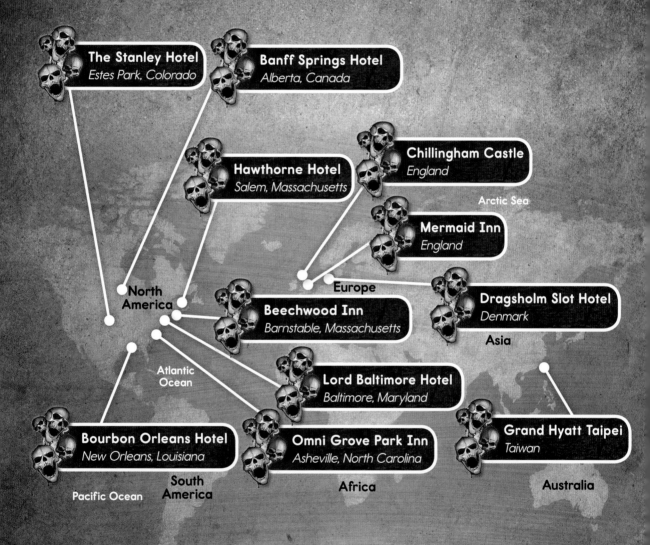

The Stanley Hotel
Estes Park, Colorado

Banff Springs Hotel
Alberta, Canada

Chillingham Castle
England

Arctic Sea

Hawthorne Hotel
Salem, Massachusetts

Mermaid Inn
England

Europe

Dragsholm Slot Hotel
Denmark

North America

Beechwood Inn
Barnstable, Massachusetts

Asia

Atlantic Ocean

Lord Baltimore Hotel
Baltimore, Maryland

Bourbon Orleans Hotel
New Orleans, Louisiana

Omni Grove Park Inn
Asheville, North Carolina

Grand Hyatt Taipei
Taiwan

South America

Africa

Australia

Pacific Ocean

Southern Ocean

SOME CHECK IN, NEVER CHECK OUT

Imagine checking into a hotel. It's late. You're tired. And just as you are ready to drift off to sleep, you see someone in your room that shouldn't be there.

Before you can blink, they disappear. Do you think your sleepy eyes are playing tricks on you? Or do you think, "Yikes! It's haunted!"

Paranormal enthusiasts and researchers love staying in hotels rumored to have ghosts.

Some hotels **capitalize** on their spooky reputations. They offer ghost tours and opportunities for guests to choose rooms that have the most reported supernatural activity.

▶▶ Some say seeing ghosts is the result of the sensed-presence effect. Darkness, fear, sleep-deprivation, and isolation can cause the brain to sense things that aren't really there.

What kinds of things happen at haunted hotels?
Who is haunting them? And why? The answers
depend on the location. Each has its own storied
history that may make them attract ghosts and
living guests, alike.

HAUNTED U.S. HOTELS

At the Beechwood Inn in Barnstable, Massachusetts, guests may be greeted politely by the spirit of an elderly woman. She is also reported to unscrew lightbulbs and bolt doors, locking people in and out. The curtains blowing when there's no wind? That's her, too.

▶▶ Paranormal researchers have investigated the Beechwood Inn. No conclusive evidence of ghost activity has been found.

But why is she there? No one knows for sure. Some think she's a spirit that fled a fire at a nearby home in the 1970s. Firemen reported seeing a ghostly **apparition** float from the burning house toward the inn.

▶▶ The woman the firefighters thought they saw was never identified. Was she really even there?

Figuring out just who might be haunting the Hawthorne Hotel in Salem, Massachusetts, is a bit easier. As the site of the 17th century Salem Witch Trials, the area might be full of restless spirits eager to **avenge** their wrongful deaths.

▶▶ The Salem Witch Trials were a series of prosecutions of people accused of witchcraft in colonial Massachusetts between 1692 and 1693.

▶▶ Hawthorne Hotel guests report feeling invisible hands touching them. Keys often go missing, and lights turn off and on by themselves.

READ IT

Some paranormal experts think if strong emotions or traumatic experiences occurred at a location, it may attract entities such as evil spirits and demons.

Some ghosts may be scary, but others may just want to have fun. At The Omni Grove Park Inn in Asheville, North Carolina, a spirit nicknamed The Pink Lady is known as quite the prankster.

▶▶ The Omni Grove Park Inn opened in 1913. The Pink Lady is reported to be the spirit of a young woman who fell from a fifth-floor balcony in the 1920s. It's said she's haunted the building ever since.

The Pink Lady shows herself as a pink mist. She likes to tickle guests' feet as they sleep. Sometimes she will hold their hands.

Some hotels have one spirit. Others have many. Ghosts from multiple **eras** are said to haunt the Bourbon Orleans Hotel in New Orleans, Louisiana.

▶▶ About 20 ghosts are said to haunt the Bourbon Orleans Hotel. Many are thought to be the spirits of children.

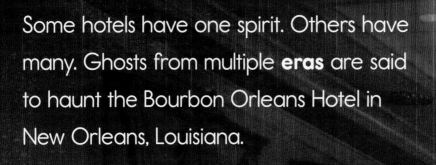

READ IT

The original building opened as the Orleans Ballroom in 1817. Masquerade balls and other events drew the area's elite. Many years and additions later, the property was sold to the Sisters of the Holy Family. From 1881 to 1864, the property was used as a convent and orphanage.

Bourbon Orleans guests claim to see the spirit of a young girl chasing a ball on the hotel's sixth floor. Others report seeing ghosts dancing in the ballroom and the apparition of a soldier.

▶▶ **The ghosts of the women and children are thought to be from the building's days as a convent and orphanage.**

It seems young spirits are just as playful in the afterlife as they are as living children. The Lord Baltimore Hotel in Baltimore, Maryland, is home to a young ghostly girl who's often seen bouncing a red ball on the hotel's 19th floor.

▶▶ The Lord Baltimore Hotel, originally built in 1928, is listed on the National Register of Historic Places.

LORD BALTIMORE HOTEL

She may not be the only ghost there, though. Guests report feeling invisible hands brush against them in the elevators and sensing a presence in their rooms. It's said the spirits also like to operate the elevators when darkness falls.

▶▶ **People familiar with the hotel say the elevators make constant trips to the 19th floor, though no one has pressed the button. No one that can be seen, anyway.**

The sounds of unseen running, giggling children echo through the halls of perhaps one of the United States' most famous haunted vacation spots: The Stanley Hotel in Estes Park, Colorado.

READ IT

After spending one night at The Stanley Hotel, Stephen King was inspired to write his best-selling novel, *The Shining*.

A housekeeper who died at the hotel in 1911 is reported to still help guests by unpacking their luggage. And the hotel's original owners, F.O. and Flora Stanley, are often seen bustling about as if they are still alive.

The Stanley Hotel is considered one of the most active paranormal sites by expert supernatural researchers.

HAUNTED HOTELS AROUND THE WORLD

The United States has more than its fair share of haunted hotels. And so does the rest of the world.

There are more than 100 reported ghosts in residence at Dragsholm Slot in Denmark. This castle built in the 12th century has hosted royalty and noblemen throughout the centuries. But the most active spirit is that of a young woman who made the mistake of falling in love.

▶▶ The Earl of Bothwell is another ghost reported to haunt the castle. Visitors claim they've seen him riding into the courtyard of the castle in his horse and carriage. The castle is now a hotel and museum.

READ IT

Construction work turned up a chilling find in the 1930s: A skeleton entombed in the brick wall.

When her father, the castle owner, discovered she was in a relationship with a man beneath her **status**, he ordered workers to brick her into a castle wall—while she was still alive.

Bodies have also been found in the thick walls of Chillingham Castle in England—those of a young boy and an older man. The discoveries were made when part of the hotel was under **renovation**.

READ IT

Some paranormal experts think renovations to a building can stir up restless spirits, perhaps because the ghost is not happy with the changes. Many accounts of hauntings start with the remodeling of a home or business.

Could the young skeleton explain the frequent appearance of the blue boy, the hotel's most famous ghost? Guests report seeing him as a blue halo near their beds.

He's not the only haunt at the Chillingham. The castle was the site of multiple gruesome executions, and the spirits of the condemned are said to remain on the property.

▶▶ **You can stay at this creepy castle any time. Be sure to check out the torture chambers and dungeons while you're there!**

The Mermaid Inn in England is **steeped** in 900 years of history, and enough reports of supernatural activity to chill the bones of the bravest guests.

One ghostly man regularly walks through the walls. Some guests awaken to a woman sitting solemnly in a chair at their bedside.

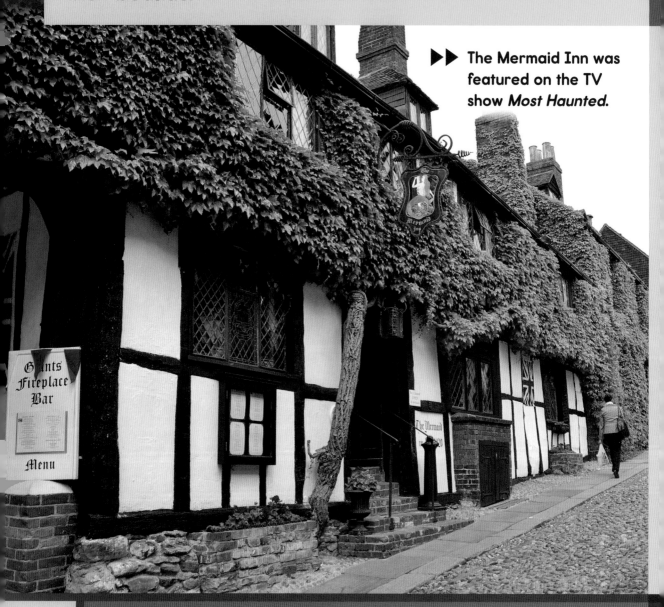

▶▶ The Mermaid Inn was featured on the TV show *Most Haunted.*

Another spirit is said to sit on the beds—once the guests are already in them, of course.

And if by chance you try to warm your clothes by the inn's fireplace, you may just find them soaking wet.

▶▶ Smugglers known as the Hawkhurst Gang frequented the hotel in the 1730s and 40s. Visitors can see the entrance to the secret passageway used by the gang.

The Banff Springs hotel in Alberta, Canada, was built more than 100 years ago as a luxury resting spot for train travelers. But tragedy has struck there more than once. A young bride is said to have fallen down the stairs after her dress caught fire. Guests report seeing her dancing in the hotel ballroom, flames flickering from her gown.

▶▶ A bellman who died in the 1970s is reported to still help hotel guests. According to the story, the man always threatened to come back and haunt the hotel.

▶▶ Sightings of the Doomed Bride, as she's known, happen in the ballroom and on the staircase.

The Grand Hyatt Hotel in Taiwan was built on land that once served as a World War II execution ground and prison camp.
The tortured souls of those who were killed are said to **manifest** themselves regularly in the hotel's rooms and hallways.

GLOSSARY

apparition (ap-uh-ri-shuhn): a ghost or ghostlike image of a person

avenge (uh-vinj): inflict harm in return for an injury or wrongdoing

capitalize (KAP-i-tuh-lize): benefit by taking advantage of something

eras (EER-uhs): long periods of time in history which have some consistent feature

manifest (MAN-uh-fest): display or show by one's acts or appearance

renovation (REN-uh-vay-shuhn): the modernization or restoration of a building

status (STAT-uhs): a person's rank or position in a group or society

steeped (steept): full of something

INDEX

YIKES! IT'S HAUNTED

VEHICLES

AUTHOR: GRACE RAMSEY

TABLE OF CONTENTS

STUDYING THE PARANORMAL

Paranormal researchers aren't just after spooky thrills. The purpose of investigations is to capture evidence that can help further our understanding of supernatural phenomena. These investigations are also done sometimes to give peace of mind to someone who thinks they are being haunted.

A good researcher will always look for a natural explanation first when investigating a reported haunting.

Want to learn more about hauntings, and the tools and methods paranormal investigators use?

Check out these websites:
http://kids.ghostvillage.com
www.scaryforkids.com/true-scary-stories

HAUNTED TRAVELS

A ship appears on the horizon, then vanishes. A man in a pilot's uniform speaks to an airline's crew moments before takeoff. Then he disappears.

An ordinary car turns into a killing machine—that seemingly can't be destroyed.

Ships, planes, and cars are used to **transport** people and cargo every day. There is nothing unusual about most of them. But when strange things happen, some people think, "Yikes! It's haunted!"

GHOST SHIPS

Reports of ghost ships are sprinkled throughout history. These aren't regular ships filled with spirits, though. The entire vessel is said to be a **phantom**.

READ IT

Paranormal research involves looking for evidence of supernatural activity, such as ghosts and hauntings. This type of activity is not explained by science or the laws of nature.

In 1748, the *Lady Lovibond* set sail to celebrate the ship captain's wedding. But not all on board were happy about the union. A jealous man steered the ship into a sandbank off the coast of England. The ship sank, killing everyone on board.

Since then, the ship is said to be spotted every 50 years, sailing around the coast. Some **witnesses** think it's in distress. They send out rescuers, but the ship cannot be found.

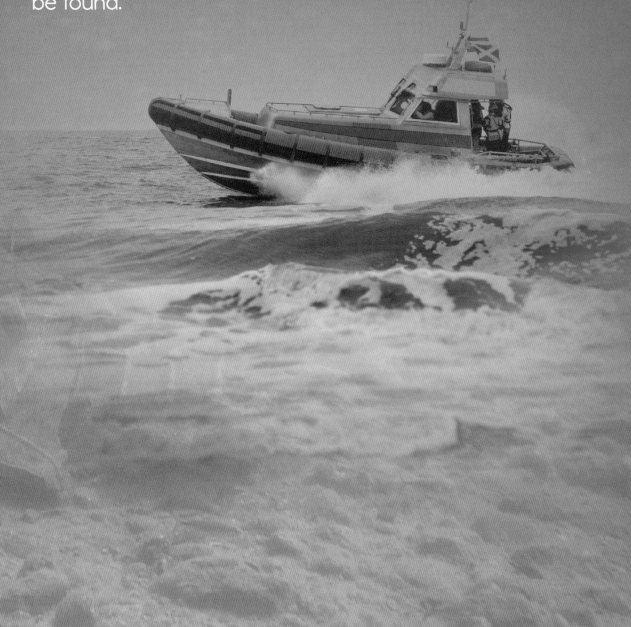

The *Palatine Light* is one of the most famous American ghost ship legends. Witnesses say the 18th century ship lights up the night near Rhode Island's Block Island. The sightings only happen during the week between Christmas and New Year's Day.

READ IT

There is no record of a ship called *Palatine* wrecking in the area. Historians think the sightings may be tied to the wreck of the Princess Augusta in 1738. When the ship ran aground near Block Island, many of the passengers and crew were sick or dead from fever. The captain refused to let the sick go ashore.

The world's most famous ghost ship tale is that of *The Flying Dutchman*. The legend began in 1641 when a Dutch ship ran into fierce storms off the coast of the Cape of Good Hope.

The ship's crew battled to get out of the storm. As the ship began to sink, the captain screamed a curse. He **vowed** to sail until doomsday.

Hundreds of fisherman and sailors have since claimed to see the ghost ship sailing the high seas.

READ IT

The lore surrounding *The Flying Dutchman* has inspired paintings, films, and books. The name can refer to both the ship and its captain.

SPOOKY SKIES

Shipwrecks aren't the only disasters that lead to haunting tales. Plane tragedies also have their own spirited stories.

READ IT

During the filming of *Casino Royale*, the movie crew refused to board a 30-year-old plane used for some scenes. Why? Because it was haunted! The jet had no power, but lights would go on and off. Some claimed to see a woman gliding through the aisle. It's said this woman died of a heart attack on board years before.

In 1977, two planes collided on a runway in Tenerife, Spain, killing 583 people. Now, some say the spirits of the victims haunt the tarmac. They appear in large numbers, waving frantically at the planes awaiting takeoff.
A warning, perhaps, of possible danger.

In 1979, American Airlines Flight 191 crashed shortly after takeoff at Chicago's O'Hare Airport. The crash killed 270 people on board and two on the ground.

▶▶ The crash of Flight 191 is among the worst plane crashes in American history.

The wreckage was cleared long ago, but the crash site was never the same. Witnesses say the temperature drops noticeably, followed by the sounds of screams from the empty field. Drivers on nearby roads report seeing strange lights and ghostly figures.

▶▶ Some nearby residents say the spirits of passengers have knocked on their doors, looking for their luggage.

Eastern Airlines Flight 401 plummeted into the Florida Everglades in 1972. The tragedy killed 101 people, including the pilot and flight engineer. But these men weren't done flying.

Parts of the wrecked plane were salvaged and fitted on other aircrafts. That's when flight crews started seeing these dedicated spirits on board. The apparitions were so well-defined, people didn't think anything of their presence.

Until the men disappeared before their eyes.

READ IT

A flight captain and two flight attendants say they spoke to one of the pilots before take-off, unaware of anything unusual. Then, they watched him vanish. They were so shaken, they canceled the flight.

EASTERN

Lockheed L1011

310

Singapore Airlines has had its own fleet of haunted jets. According to reports, crew members were petrified when assigned to a few of the airline's 747s. Angry ghosts were said to stalk the aisles, sometimes throwing silverware.

SINISTER CARS

Like planes, sometimes wrecked cars are salvaged for usable parts. Sometimes those parts seem to be bad luck, at best. Some say they are cursed.

Movie star James Dean was excited about his new Porsche 550 Spyder. But a friend told him to get rid of it, or he would be dead in a week. The man got a **sinister** feeling from the car. Dean's girlfriend refused to get in it. Others warned him, as well, according to the legend of the "Death Car."

A week later, Dean died in a head-on collision. Parts of the mangled Spyder were installed in another race car. The driver hit a tree and died instantly.

READ IT

Dean's wrecked car was stored in a garage at one time. The garage caught fire, burning to the ground. The car was untouched by the flames.

U.S. President John F. Kennedy (1917-1963) was assassinated in his 1961 Lincoln 74A convertible on a November afternoon. The car was modified and kept in service after his death, until it was retired to the Henry Ford Museum in 1978.

An apparition is said to appear near the car, especially in November.

Archduke Franz Ferdinand of Austria (1863-1914) and his wife were shot by an assassin as they sat in their limousine. The archduke's death launched World War I. Over the next 20 years, the limo was owned by fifteen people. It was involved in six accidents and thirteen deaths. Some say the vehicle is cursed.

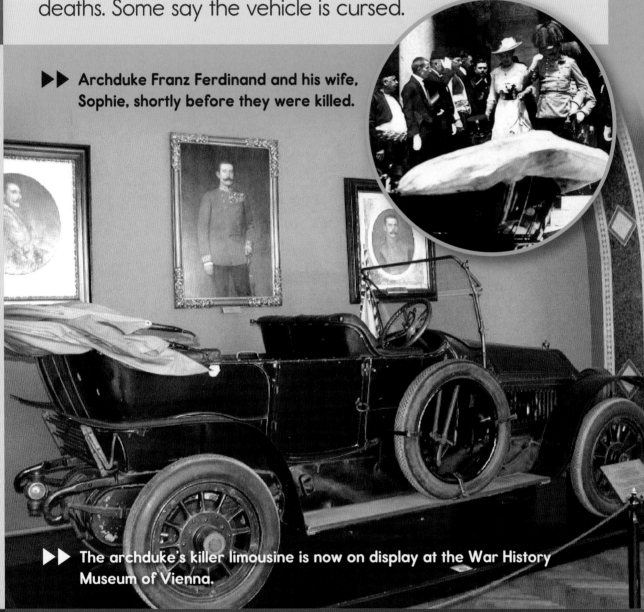

▶▶ Archduke Franz Ferdinand and his wife, Sophie, shortly before they were killed.

▶▶ The archduke's killer limousine is now on display at the War History Museum of Vienna.

What turns something ordinary like a car or plane into something spooky? Some think spirits can attach themselves to objects that were part of their death. Some think it's possible for unhuman **entities**, such as demons, to attach themselves to ordinary objects.

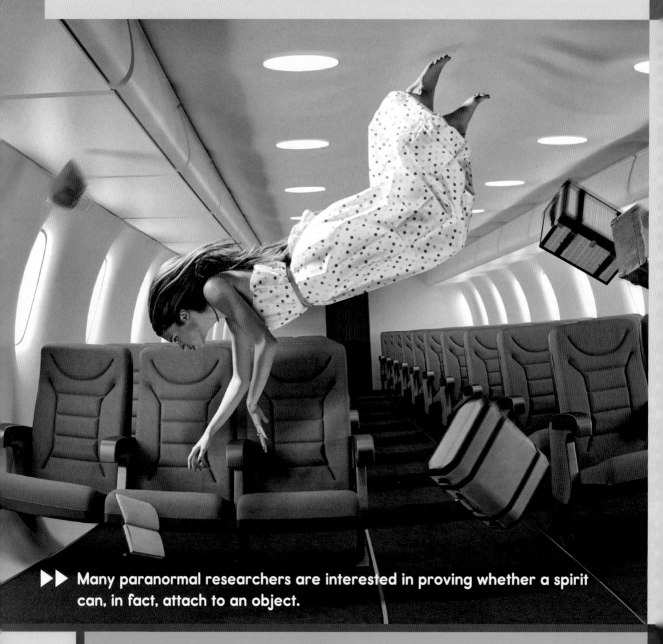

▶▶ Many paranormal researchers are interested in proving whether a spirit can, in fact, attach to an object.

Some people think ghost ships **manifest** from the energy left behind by tragic shipwrecks.

Traumatic events are thought to leave imprints on a location. Some say these imprints play over and over, like a movie on repeat.

Skeptics say ghost ships are simply mirages. They think ghost sightings are people's minds playing tricks on them. Can ships, planes, and cars really be haunted?

What do you believe?

GLOSSARY

entities (IN-tuh-tees): things with distinct and independent existences

manifest (MAN-uh-fest): display or show by one's acts or appearance

paranormal (PAR-uh-nor-muhl): events or phenomena that are beyond the scope of normal scientific understanding

phantom (FAN-tuhm): a ghost

skeptics (SKEP-ticks): people who doubt the truth or validity of a claim or belief

sinister (SIN-iss-tuhr): giving the impression that something harmful or evil is happening or will happen

transport (tran-SPORT): take or carry people or goods from one place to another

vowed (vowd): solemnly promised to do a specified thing

witnesses (WIT-nis-ehs): people who see an event, typically a crime or accident, take place

INDEX

YIKES! IT'S HAUNTED

OBJECTS

AUTHOR: GRACE RAMSEY

TABLE OF CONTENTS

STUDYING THE PARANORMAL

Paranormal researchers aren't just after spooky thrills. The purpose of investigations is to capture evidence that can help further our understanding of supernatural phenomena. These investigations are also done sometimes to give peace of mind to someone who thinks they are being haunted. Using tools such as EMF meters, motion sensors, and laser grids, researchers try to collect evidence that they might have missed with a simple camera. Want to learn more about hauntings, and the tools and methods paranormal investigators use?

Check out these websites:
https://www.cbc.ca/kidscbc2/the-feed/monsters-101-all-about-ghosts
http://www.destinationamerica.com/thehauntist/9-fascinating-ghost-hunting-tools-you-should-know-more-about-2/

▶▶ Paranormal researchers always get permission before investigating a property.

STRANGE OBJECTS

Normally, dolls need people to move them. Chairs do nothing but sit still. And paintings simply hang on walls without any effect on their environments.

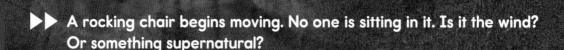

▶▶ A rocking chair begins moving. No one is sitting in it. Is it the wind? Or something supernatural?

But when these and other objects behave strangely, some people think, "Yikes! It's haunted!"

READ IT

Paranormal research involves looking for evidence of supernatural activity. This type of activity is not explained by science or the laws of nature.

Throughout history, there have been many claims of haunted objects. Some think spirits can attach themselves to objects that were significant to them in life.

Some think it's possible for unhuman **entities**, such as demons, to attach themselves to ordinary objects.

▶▶ People who claim to experience hauntings sometimes say their TVs and other electronics turn on and off on their own.

PARANORMAL PLAYTHINGS

Dolls are beloved by children all over the world. But sometimes these toys get bad **reputations**.

Some dolls, for example, have been examined after extraordinary events were blamed on their presence. These dolls are thought to be cursed or **possessed** by a spirit.

Mandy, a doll made in the early 1900s, cried every night, according to the woman who owned it. The sound of its wails echoed through the childless house, waking its owner, who finally gave the doll away.

READ IT

In the late 1800s, a young boy received a handmade doll from a family servant. Soon, strange things began happening. Objects were thrown across the room. Other toys were destroyed. Family members felt threatened. The boy began insisting that his family call him by his middle name, Gene, because the doll was the real Robert. He also insisted Robert was to blame for all the bad things that happened. Robert is now on display at East Martello Museum in Key West, Florida. Robert's legend grew more famous after the *Child's Play* film series was based on it.

Mandy is now kept in a glass case at Quesnel & District Museum in Canada. The staff says the doll bangs on the glass and will destroy any doll that is placed near it.
The crying stopped at the home once Mandy was gone.

SPIRITED FURNITURE

You can probably look around and see at least one chair right now. You may even be sitting in one. What if that chair was haunted?

The chairs at Belcourt Castle in Rhode Island don't welcome visitors with open arms. An icy chill is felt by those who dare to get close to them. People who try to sit on them claim to encounter **resistance** from an unseen force.

▶▶ Banquet Hall at Belcourt Castle

▶▶ Belcourt Castle is also reported to house a haunted mirror, a possessed statue, and a screaming suit of armor.

The Busby Stoop Chair, owned by convicted murderer Thomas Busby, is rumored to be cursed by his **vengeful** spirit. The chair remained in the Busby Inn after he was hanged for his crime in the 1700s.

People who sat in the chair were often involved in **fatal** accidents. In 1978, the chair was moved to the Thirsk Museum in North Yorkshire.

No one has sat in it since.

IF WALLS COULD TALK

Mirror, mirror on the wall, who's behind me in the hall?

▶▶ Many plantations are said to be haunted, or contain haunted objects, due to their history of slavery and the intense negative energy left behind.

When you're brushing your teeth in the morning, you don't expect to see anyone other than your family appear in the mirror around you.

READ IT

A mirror at the Roosevelt Hotel in Hollywood, California, is rumored to be haunted by the legendary Marilyn Monroe. Guests and staff say they see her reflection looking back at them.

At the Myrtles Plantation in Louisiana, you may catch a glimpse of the spirits rumored to be stuck inside its famous mirror.

▶▶ **The plantation, built in 1796, now operates as a bed & breakfast and hosts daily tours.**

READ IT

The Myrtles Plantation is considered one of America's most haunted houses. Many deaths occurred there. Photographs of the mirror appear to show multiple handprints, which seem to come from the opposite side of the glass. The glass has been cleaned and replaced, but the handprints still appear.

In some cultures, people cover the mirrors in a home when someone passes away. This is done so the deceased's soul will not be trapped inside one.

▶▶ Paranormal enthusiasts come from all over to stay at the plantation, hoping to experience its reported hauntings.

When you think of art, do you think of ghosts? Most people don't. But there are a few works of art that have scared up spirited rumors.

Some paintings are said to come to life in the night. Others bring spirits into the homes where they hang.

▶▶ The internet is teeming with stories of haunted paintings. Some have been blamed for causing illness and death.

READ IT

The Anguished Man was an unwanted gift. It was considered evil and kept stored away. When the original owner died, her grandson took the painting to his home. He didn't believe there was anything to the stories his grandmother told.

Shortly afterward, the man and his wife began seeing a shadow figure in their home. They also heard crying from a corner of a room. The painting has traveled to many reportedly haunted locations, where paranormal investigators say it has interacted with other spirits.

The Crying Boy is said to set homes ablaze. In several accounts of destroyed homes all over Europe, firefighters sifting through the rubble have found a copy of this late 1960s painting of a young boy with a tear rolling down his cheek.

In each case, the portrait is unharmed, though the house is burned to the ground.

SPOOKY THREADS

There's a wedding dress in Pennsylvania that witnesses say shakes and sways in its glass case. The dress was picked out by young Anna Baker, before her father forbid her to marry the man she loved. Anna never married.

▶▶ The Baker Mansion is a historic home in Pennsylvania built between 1844 and 1848.

She died in the family home in 1914. The home became a museum, and the dress was put on display. According to some accounts, the dress shakes so violently, museum staff fear it might break the glass.

▶▶ Visitors and staff claim they've seen the ghosts of both Anna and her father in the mansion.

WHAT CAUSES A HAUNTING?

Objects believed to be haunted can be new or old. They can be works of art, tools, chests, jewelry, and even toys. But what turns an ordinary, everyday object into something spooky?

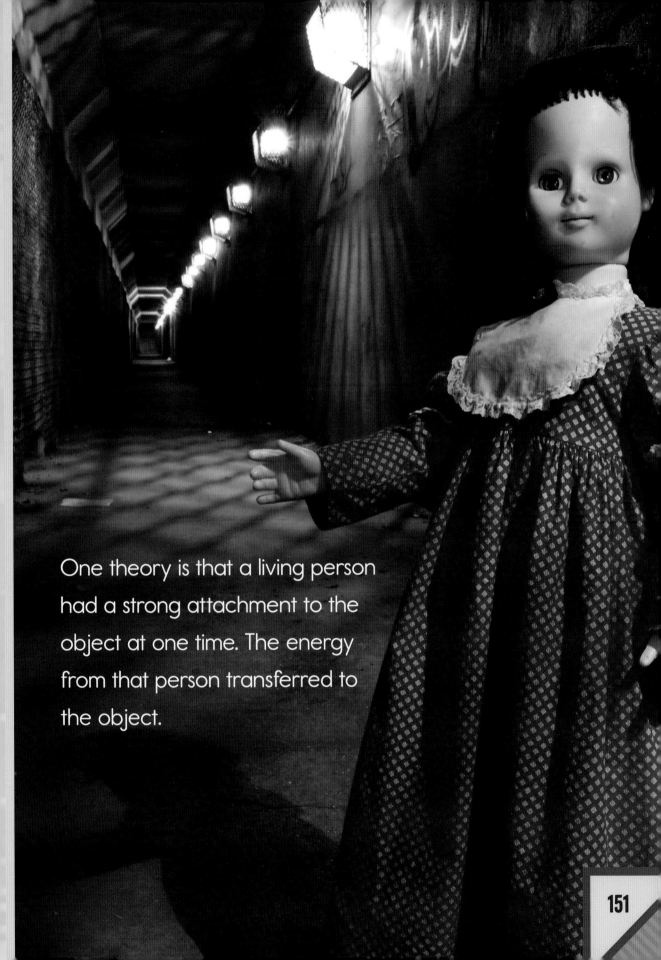

One theory is that a living person had a strong attachment to the object at one time. The energy from that person transferred to the object.

If the energy was negative, or the person was violent, the hauntings take on a more **sinister** nature.

Can objects really be haunted? Or might overactive imaginations be responsible for reports of paranormal activity?

What do you *believe?*

▶▶ Haunted objects are often sold to collectors. In 2015, a man auctioned a laptop he claimed was possessed after leaving it at a graveyard overnight.

GLOSSARY

entities (IN-tuh-tees): things with distinct and independent existences

fatal (FAY-tuhl): causing or leading to death

paranormal (PAR-uh-nor-muhl): events or phenomena that are beyond the scope of normal scientific understanding

possessed (PUH-zest): controlled by an evil spirit

reputations (rep-yuh-TAY-shuhns): worth or character as judged by others

resistance (ri-ZIS-tuhns): the act of resisting or fighting back; a force that opposes the motion of an object

sinister (SIN-iss-tuhr): giving the impression that something harmful or evil is happening or will happen

vengeful (venj-full): seeking to harm someone in return for a perceived injury

INDEX

YIKES! IT'S HAUNTED

HOUSES

AUTHOR: ALEX SUMMERS

TABLE OF CONTENTS

HAUNTED HOUSES OF THE WORLD

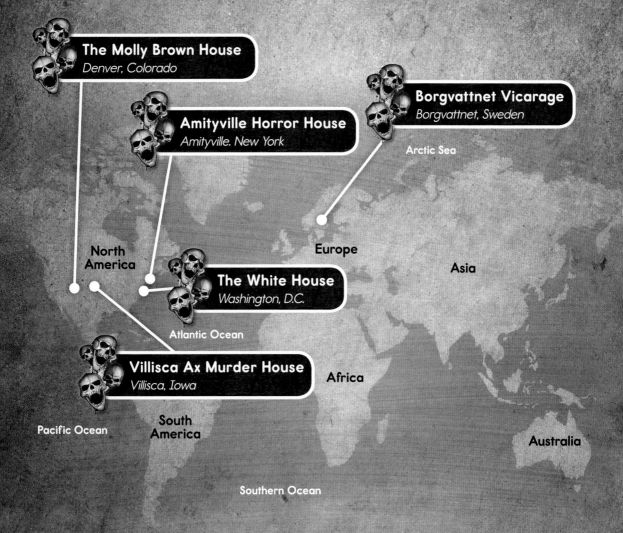

The Molly Brown House
Denver, Colorado

Amityville Horror House
Amityville. New York

Borgvattnet Vicarage
Borgvattnet, Sweden

Arctic Sea

North America

Europe

Asia

The White House
Washington, D.C.

Atlantic Ocean

Villisca Ax Murder House
Villisca, Iowa

Africa

Pacific Ocean

South America

Australia

Southern Ocean

STRANGE SENSATIONS

Do you ever feel like someone is watching you, but there's no one there? No one you can see, anyway.

Cold spots, unexplained noises, and the sense you're not alone in a house can make you think, "Yikes! It's haunted!" Hauntings are reported at homes all over the world—including the U.S. president's home.

READ IT

Paranormal, or supernatural, activity is not explained by science or the laws of nature. A haunting is considered a supernatural occurrence.

HAUNTED WHITE HOUSE

The White House is haunted? **Rumor** is 1600 Pennsylvania Avenue in Washington, D.C., the most famous U.S. address, is teeming with paranormal activity.

The most frequently reported sighting in the White House is the ghost, or spirit, of the 16th president, Abraham Lincoln.

His wife, Mary, held many **séances** in the White House, which the president attended. Lincoln was said to have predicted his own death more than once before it happened.

President Lincoln's life was cut **tragically** short by an **assassin's** bullet in April 1865. His spirit may remain as a result of his traumatic demise.

ASSASSINATION OF PRESIDENT LINCOLN, FORD'S THEATRE, WASHINGTON, APRIL 14, 1865.

READ IT

Other presidents, such as Harry Truman and Andrew Jackson, make ghostly appearances to White House visitors, as well.

AMITYVILLE HORROR HOUSE

112 Ocean Avenue, in Amityville, N.Y. is not a place you want to visit alone, or maybe at all!

▶▶ Ronald DeFeo Jr. testified that he heard voices, which told him to murder his family.

In 1974, six members of the DeFeo family were killed in that house by their oldest son. The following year it was sold, but it did not come unoccupied.

▶▶ **Police divers search the family swimming pool for the .35 caliber Marlin rifle allegedly used by Ronald (Butch) DeFeo to murder his father, mother, and four younger siblings.**

The new owners, George and Kathy Lutz, reported a tormented ghost who ripped doors from hinges and slammed cabinets. They also reported seeing demonic faces and swarms of insects inside the house. Yikes!

They recounted their story to a writer named Jay Anson, who published *The Amityville Horror: A True Story*, in 1977.

READ IT

The book became a best-seller, followed by a film that sparked nearly a half-dozen sequels. This horrifying story spooked millions of people. But is it true?

▶▶ Actor Ryan Reynolds played George Lutz in the 2005 movie based on the horrifying experiences the family endured after purchasing what they thought would be their "dream home."

VILLISCA AX MURDER HOUSE

On Thursday, June 13, 1912, two adults and six children were found **brutally** murdered in their beds in the small mid-western town of Villisca, Iowa.

The murders were never solved, and a sense of gloom still **lingers** in the home. Many believe that the spirits of the murdered family still remain here, their ghosts haunting the old house where they tragically died.

▶▶ We will never know what happened that dark night inside the home of J.B. and Sarah Moore. Given the many years that have passed, the killer's dark secret was carried to their own grave.

Tours of the home have been cut short by falling lamps, moving objects, and banging sounds. Some psychics have claimed to communicate with the spirits of the dead there.

▶▶ **A pan of bloody water was discovered on the kitchen table as well as a plate of uneaten food.**

▶▶ **It is believed that sometime between midnight and 5 a.m., an unknown assailant entered the home of J.B. Moore and brutally murdered all occupants of the house with an ax.**

Paranormal investigators and thrill-seekers who have stayed overnight claim they were awoken by the sounds of children's voices. Others have captured mysterious audio, video, and photographic evidence suggesting something supernatural lurks within the walls.

BORGVATTNET
(THE HAUNTED VICARAGE)

Moving objects, screams, shadow people, and an old rocking chair that keeps rocking?

The Borgvattnet **Vicarage** is said to be one of Sweden's most haunted houses, and you can expect all these things and more to happen here.

READ IT

One resident of the home claimed that he could not sit in the rocking chair for long, because an unseen force would always throw him out of it.

In the early 1980s, a priest named Tore Forslund attempted to perform an exorcism on the house. It was unsuccessful.

▶▶ The first documented account of paranormal activity at the vicarage happened in 1927, when a resident chaplain reported that he witnessed his laundry being torn down from the line by an unseen force in the attic.

The vicarage is now a bed and breakfast for those curious enough to stay the night. Anyone who makes it through the night receives a diploma to mark their bravery.

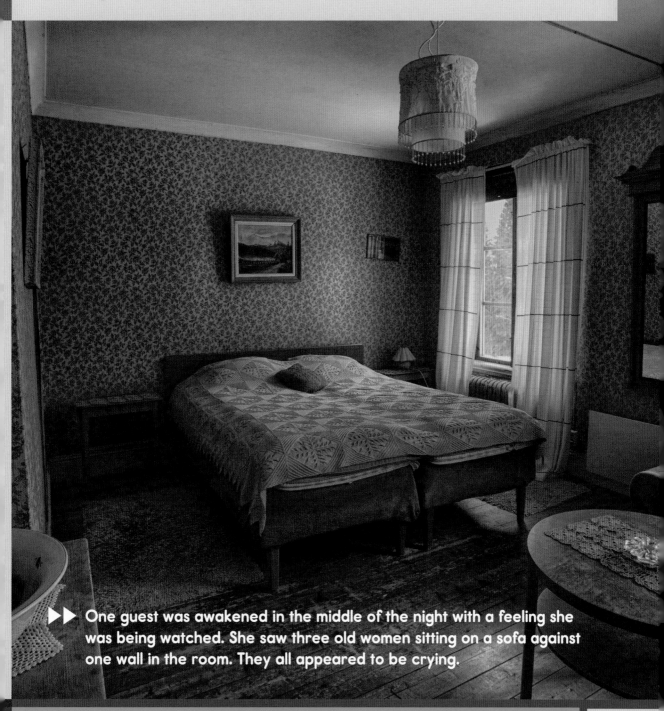

▶▶ One guest was awakened in the middle of the night with a feeling she was being watched. She saw three old women sitting on a sofa against one wall in the room. They all appeared to be crying.

THE MOLLY BROWN HOUSE

The Molly Brown House is in Denver, Colorado. Molly died in 1932 and soon after. . . well, let's just say Molly never really left. At least not her ghostly form.

An apparition of a woman in a long dress is often seen sitting at the dining room table. She is also known to rearrange the chairs.

▶▶ Public tours are held at the Molly Brown House. If you're lucky, you may spot some apparitions, or hear some phantom piano music.

Visitors sometimes report smelling pipe smoke in the attic and the basement. This is where J.J. Brown, Molly's husband, might have snuck down to smoke his pipe—away from his disapproving wife.

READ IT

The Molly Brown House now operates as a museum, and many paranormal experiences still occur here. Not only do Molly and J.J. seem to be haunting the house, but there are several others as well. Molly's mother, who also lived in the home, has been seen peering out her window.

WHAT CAUSES A HAUNTING?

Many haunted houses are very old with a lot of history. Births, deaths, traumatic events, and strong emotions have occurred in these homes.

But what turns an ordinary, everyday house into something spooky?

Believers in the paranormal think hauntings happen for different reasons. Sometimes when a spirit appears it is to say goodbye to a loved one. Other times, a ghost may have more sinister intentions.

▶▶ **An earthbound spirit may have died so quickly that they are unaware of being dead.**

One theory about hauntings is that they are imprints left in the Earth's energy field. Some scientists accept that brain waves emit an electrical field that can affect and enhance spirit activity.

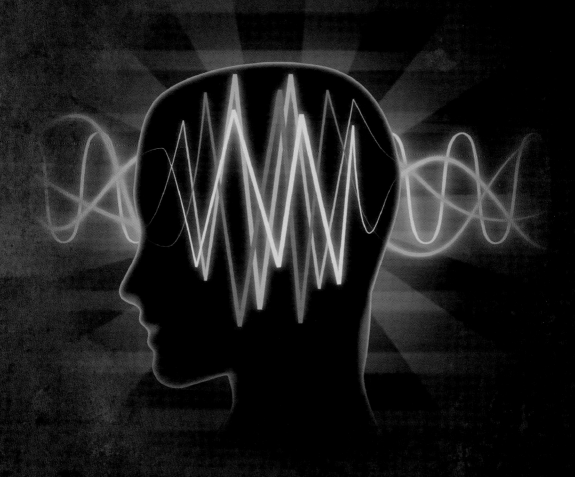

▶▶ Spirits are thought to remain as trapped energy. In this condition, they may attach to a living person's energy field.

Some people think the **residual** energy from a deceased person may linger in a home, especially if they died there with unfinished business. This may compel the person's spirit to continue to reach out to the living.

Or if something terrible happened in a home, dark or evil spirits may be drawn there by the negative energy created by that event.

What do you *believe?*

GLOSSARY

assassins (uh-SAS-uhnz): people hired to murder someone who is well-known or famous

brutally (BRUH-tuhl-ee): to do something in an extremely cruel or violent way

lingers (LING-uhrz): being slow in leaving or continuing to stay

residual (RUH-zi-dyoo-uhl): the remains of something left over

rumor (ROO-mur): a story that is spread by mouth but may not be true

séances (SAY-ahn-siz): meetings where people try to contact the dead

tragically (TRAJ-ik-lee): when someone has died or suffered in a shocking or cruel way

vicarage (vik-uhr-ij): the residence or home of a vicar, or holy man such as a priest

INDEX

SHOW WHAT YOU KNOW

GRAVEYARDS

1. What spooky occurrences can you expect on a visit to Fort Meigs?
2. What are considered to be the most haunted parts of Castillo de San Marcos?
3. Why do ghosts reveal themselves to all sorts of people?
4. Who haunts Highgate Cemetery in the United Kingdom?
5. What is Howard Street Cemetery most famous for?

PRISONS

1. Name a form of punishment used by prison guards to get inmates to confess or cooperate.
2. After the Willard Asylum closed, what was found in the attic?
3. Name two things that might bind a spirit or ghost to a place.
4. How long was Beechworth Lunatic Asylum in operation?
5. What increases the chances of a place being haunted?

HOTELS

1. What is paranormal activity?
2. What does a good paranormal researcher do?
3. Why do you think so many hotels are considered haunted?
4. Would you stay at a hotel that's supposedly haunted?
5. What made The Stanley Hotel so famous? Do you think this affected how people felt about the hotel?

VEHICLES

1. Why might a traumatic event lead to a haunting?
2. What might a skeptic think causes people to believe in hauntings?
3. Why did people warn James Dean about driving his new car?
4. Why do you think people are inspired to create art and stories about *The Flying Dutchman*?
5. Why might the airline pilot and engineer of Flight 401 still appear to people on planes?

OBJECTS

1. What are some reasons people think an object can be haunted?

2. What reasons do believers think might lead a spirit to attach to an object?

3. Is it possible for a new object to be haunted?

4. What kind of object do you think is the creepiest?

5. What do you think about ghosts and hauntings? Are they real or imagined?

HOUSES

1. Name one thing that may cause a house to be haunted.

2. What are some things you might expect to see at the Borgvattnet Vicarage?

3. How many people were murdered at the Villisca Ax Murder House?

4. Do you believe in the paranormal? Why or why not?

5. Where is the Amityville House located? What made it so famous?

MEET THE AUTHORS

ABOUT THE AUTHOR

Alex Summers loves all things paranormal. From a distance, that is! She was born in St. Augustine, Florida, not far from Castillo de San Marcos, and still visits there every chance she gets. She has even done a paranormal tour of the fort and has picked up EVPs in some of the haunted areas. In her spare time she loves to read and watch anything having to do with hauntings and ghosts. Then she sleeps with the lights on!

HOUSES

PRISONS

GRAVEYARDS

ABOUT THE AUTHOR

Grace Ramsey is a journalist, author, and mega-fan of paranormal research shows. She once joined a crew of investigators at one of the world's most haunted places. Her experiences there made her much less skeptical of the supernatural. She still gets the chills just thinking about that night. Yikes!

Meet The Author!
www.meetREMauthors.com

OBJECTS

HOTELS

VEHICLES

PHOTO CREDITS

Cover/ Title Page © Don Cline; Pages 4-5 © Linux87; Page 6 © EricVega; Page 7 © William Attard McCarthy; Page 8 © JayLazarin; Page 9 © johnnorth; Page 10 © Burchin Tuncer; Page 11 © chrisdorney; Page 12 © James Lemire; Page 13 Hulton Archive, Bob Harrison; Page 14 © Benkrut; Page 15 © Appalachianviews; Page 16 © Wikipedia; Page 17 © Tribune Content Agency LLC / Alamy Stock Photo ; Pages 18-19 © FloNight (Sydney Poore) and Russell Poore; Page 20 © Nadya Lukic; Page 21 © Paul Giamou; Page 22 © ZORAN IVANOVIC; Page 23 © Erin Cadigan; Page 24 © bonciutoma; Pages 25, 28 © Redrockschool; Page 26 © Ferran Traité Soler; Page 27 © inhauscreative

Cover/Title Page/Page 15 © Nagel Photography; Pages 4-5 © Zanico; Page 6 © Corepics VOF; Page 7 © canjoena; Page 8 © Tim Kiser; Page 9 © VitaleBaby; Page 10 © Jim West / Alamy Stock Photo; Page 11 © Nadya Lukic; Page 12 © Gary Whitton; Page 13 © Zack Frank; Page 14 © LOU OATES; Pages 16,17,19 © Stephen King Photography; Page 18 © Jeff Thrower; Pages 20-23 © Jennifer Morrisey; Page 24 © Lario Tus; Page 25 © albund; Page 26-27 © Butriano; Page 27 © Elnur; Page 28 © Taylor Hinton